MW00886157

CONTENTS

A Pond Full of Milk

Once upon a time, there was a king called Bobo. He told his workers to dig a pond inside his castle.

Once the pond was dug, Bobo made an announcement to his people saying that one person from each household has to bring a jug of milk during the night and pour it into the pond. So, the pond should  be full of milk by the morning and the King can then distribute the milk to those in need in the country.

After receiving the order, everyone went home. Wawa prepared to bring the milk to the castle during the night. He thought that since everyone will bring milk, he could just bring a glass of water and pour it into the pond. Because it will be dark at night, no one will even notice. So he swiftly went to the castle and poured some water into the pond and came back.

In the morning, King Bobo went to visit the pond and to his astonishment, the pond was full, but it was filled with water!

What happened is that everyone was thinking like Wawa that "I don't have to pour any milk, someone else will do it."

Dear children, when it comes to helping the country, don't think that others will take care of it. Rather, it starts from each of you. If you don't do it, no one else will do it. So, do your job and that will make a difference to our country.

This story teaches us: be responsible and do your job.

DON'T CHANGE THE WORLD

Once upon a time, there was a king who ruled a prosperous country. One day, he went for a trip to some distant areas of his country. When he was back to his palace, he complained that his feet were very painful, because it was the first time that he went for such a long trip, and the road that he went through was very rough and stony. He then ordered his people to cover every road of the entire country with leather.

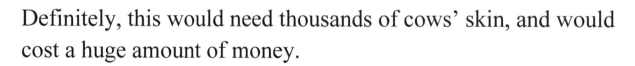

Definitely, this would need thousands of cows' skin, and would cost a huge amount of money.

Then one of his wise servants dared himself to tell the king, "Why do you have to spend that unnecessary amount of money?

Why don't you just cut a little piece of leather to cover your feet?"

The king was surprised, but he later agreed to his suggestion, to make a "shoe" for himself.

There is actually a valuable lesson of life in this story: to make this world a happy place to live, you better change yourself - your heart; and not the world.

THE TRAVELERS AND THE PLANE TREE

Two men were walking along one summer day. Soon it became too hot to go any further and, seeing a large plane tree nearby, they threw themselves on the ground to rest in its shade. Gazing up into the branches one man said to the other:

"What a useless tree this is. It does not have fruit or nuts that we can eat and we cannot even use its wood for anything.

"Don't be so ungrateful," rustled the tree in reply. "I am being extremely useful to you at this very moment, shielding you from the hot sun. And you call me a good-for-nothing!"

All of God's creations have a good purpose. Islam teaches us that we should never belittle Allah's blessings.

LEARN FROM MISTAKES

Thomas Edison tried two thousand different materials in search of a filament for the light bulb. When none worked satisfactorily, his assistant complained, "All our work is in vain. We have learned nothing."

Edison replied very confidently, "Oh, we have come a long way and we have learned a lot. We now know that there are two thousand elements which we cannot use to make a good light bulb."

THE BOY WHO CRIED 'WOLF'

Once there was a shepherd boy who had to look after a flock of sheep. One day, he felt bored and decided to play a trick on the villagers. He shouted, "Help! Wolf! Wolf!"

The villagers heard his cries and rushed out of the village to help the shepherd boy. When they reached him, they asked,

"Where is the wolf?"

The shepherd boy laughed loudly, "Ha, Ha, Ha! I fooled all of you. I was only playing a trick on you."

A few days later, the shepherd boy played this trick again.

Again he cried, "Help! Help! Wolf! Wolf!" Again, the villagers rushed up the hill to help him and again they found that boy had tricked them. They were very angry with him for being so naughty.

Then, sometime later, a wolf went into the field. The wolf attacked one sheep, and then another and another. The

shepherd boy ran towards the village shouting, "Help! Help! Wolf! Help! Somebody!"

The villagers heard his cries but they laughed because they thought it was another trick. The boy ran to the nearest villager and said, "A wolf is attacking the sheep. I lied before, but this time it is true!"

Finally, the villagers went to look. It was true. They could see the wolf running away and many dead sheep lying on the grass.

We may not believe someone who often tells lies, even when he tells the truth.

THE FARMER AND THE STORK

Finding that cranes were destroying his newly sown corn, a farmer one evening set a net in his field to catch the destructive birds. When he went to examine the net next morning he found a number of cranes and also a stork.

"Release me, I beseech you," cried the stork, "for I have eaten none of your corn, nor have I done you any harm. I am a poor innocent stork, as you may see - a most dutiful

bird, I honor my father and mother. I..."

But the farmer cut him short. "All this may be true enough, I dare say, but I have caught you with those were destroying my crops, and you must suffer with the company in which you are found."

People are judged by the company they keep.

THE HARE AND THE TORTOISE

A tortoise one day met a hare who made fun of her. "My, my, you move so slowly, you will never get far!" The tortoises, upset by the hare's manner, said,
"Let's have a race and see who is faster."

The hare laughed and said,
"You must be joking! But all right, we'll see who reaches the other side of the hill first."
Off he ran, leaving the tortoise far behind.

After a while, the hare stopped to wait for the tortoise to come long. He waited and waited till he felt

sleepy. "I might as well take a nap," he thought. "Even if she catches up with me, I can easily win the race." So he lay down under a shady tree and closed his eyes.

When the tortoise passed the sleeping hare, she walked on slowly but steadily. By the time the hare woke up, the tortoise was near the finishing line. He ran as fast as he could, but he could not catch up with the tortoise.

Slow and steady can win the race.

THE ANT AND THE DOVE

One hot day, an ant was searching for some water. After walking around for some time, she came to a spring.
To reach the spring, she had to climb up a blade of grass. While making her way up, she slipped and fell into the water.

She could have drowned if a dove up a nearby tree had not seen her. Seeing that the ant was in trouble, the dove quickly plucked off a leaf and dropped it into the water near the struggling ant. The ant moved towards the leaf and climbed up there. Soon it carried her safely to dry ground.

Just at that time, a hunter nearby was throwing out his net towards the dove, hoping to trap it.

Guessing what he was about to do, the ant quickly bit him on the heel. Feeling the pain, the hunter dropped his net. The dove was quick to fly away to safety.

One good turn deserves another.

THE MONKEY AND THE DOLPHIN

One day long ago, some sailors set out to sea in their sailing ship. One of them brought his pet monkey along for the long journey.

When they were far out at sea, a terrible storm overturned their ship. Everyone fell into the sea, and the monkey was sure that he would drown.

Suddenly a dolphin appeared and picked him up. They soon reached the island and the monkey came down from the dolphin's back. The dolphin asked the monkey, "Do you know this place?"

The monkey replied, "Yes, I do. In fact, the king of the island is my best friend. Do you know that I am actually a prince?" Knowing that no one lived on the island, the dolphin said, "Well, well, so you are a prince! Now you can be a king!"

The monkey asked, "How can I be a king?"
As the dolphin started swimming away, he answered, "That is easy. As you are the only creatures on this island, you will naturally be the king!"

Those who lie and boast may end up in trouble.

THE FOX AND THE STORK

A selfish fox once invited a stork to dinner at his home in a hollow tree. That evening, the stork flew to the fox's home and knocked on the door with her long beak. The fox opened the door and said, "Please come in and share my food."
The stork was invited to sit down at the table. She was very hungry and the food smelled delicious! The fox served soup in shallow bowls and he licked up all his soup very quickly. However, the stork could not have any of it as the bowl was too

shallow for her long beak. The poor stork just smiled politely and stayed hungry.

The selfish fox asked, "Stork, why haven't you taken your soup? Don't you like it?"

The stork replied, "It was very kind of you to invite me for dinner. Tomorrow evening, please join me for dinner at my home." The next day, when the fox arrived at the stork's home, he saw that they were also having soup for dinner. This time the soup was served in tall jugs. The stork drank the soup easily but the fox could not reach inside the tall jug. This time it was his turn to go hungry.

A selfish act can backfire on you.

THE WOLF AND THE LAMB

A lamb was grazing with a flock of sheep one day. She soon found some sweet grass at the edge of the field. Farther and farther she went away from the others. She was enjoying herself so much that she did not notice a wolf coming nearer to her.

However, when it pounced on her, she was quick to start pleading, "Please, please don't eat me yet. My stomach is full of grass. If you wait a while, I will taste much better."

The wolf thought that was a good idea, so he sat down and waited. After a while, the lamb said, "If you allow me to dance, the grass in my stomach will be digested faster." Again the wolf agreed.
While the lamb was dancing, she had a new

idea. She said, "Please take the bell from around my neck. If you ring it as hard as you can, I will be able to dance even faster."

The wolf took the bell and rang it as hard as he could. The shepherd heard the bell ringing and quickly sent his dogs to find the missing lamb. The barking dogs frightened the wolf away and saved the lamb's life.

The gentle and weak can sometimes be cleverer than fierce and strong.

THE FOX AND THE GRAPES

It was a sunny day and fox was walking across the fields. Soon he came to a vineyard. As he came nearer, he could see some bunches of juicy grapes. The fox looked carefully around him. He had to make sure that he was safe from the hunters. He decided to steal some before anyone came along. He jumped upwards but he could not reach the grapes. He jumped again as high as he could. He still could not reach them. The grapes were just too high for him!

He was not ready to give up. He backed off, took some running steps and leapt into the air towards the grapes. Again he failed to reach them.

It was getting dark, and he was getting angry. His legs hurt with all that running and jumping. At last he stopped trying.
As he walked away, he said to himself, "I don't really want those grapes. I'm sure they are too sour to eat."

Sometimes when we cannot get what we want, we pretend that it is not worth having.

THE THIRSTY CROW

One hot day, a thirsty crow flew all over the fields looking for water. For a long time, she could not find any. She felt very weak, almost giving up hope.

Suddenly, she saw a water jug below her. She flew straight down to see if there was any water inside. Yes, she could see some water inside the jug!
The crow tried to push her head into the jug. Sadly, she found that the neck of the jug was too narrow. Then she tried to push the jug down for the water to flow out. She found that the jug was too heavy.

The crow thought hard for a while. Then looking around her, she saw some pebbles. She suddenly had a good idea. She started picking up the pebbles one by one, dropping each into the jug.

As more and more pebbles filled the jug, the water level kept rising. Soon it was high enough for the crow to drink. Her plan had worked!

If you try hard enough, you may soon find an answer to your problem.

THE MILKMAID

A milkmaid was on her way to the market to sell some milk from her cow. As she carried the large jug of milk on top of her head, she began to dream of all the things she could do after selling the milk.

"With that money, I'll buy a hundred chicks to rear in my backyard. When they are fully grown, I can sell them at a good price at the market."

As she walked on, she continued dreaming, "Then I'll buy two young goats and rear them on the grass close by. When they are fully grown, I can sell them at an even better price!"

Still dreaming, she said to herself, "Soon, I'll be able to buy another cow, and I will have more milk to sell. Then I shall have even more money..."

With these happy thoughts, she began to skip and jump. Suddenly she tripped and fell. The jug broke and all the milk spilt onto the ground.

No more dreaming now, she sat down and cried.

Do not count your chickens before they are hatched.

PARABLE OF THE PENCIL

The Pencil Maker took the pencil aside, just before putting him into the box.
"There are 5 things you need to know," he told the pencil,
"Before I send you out into the world. Always remember them and never forget, and you will become the best pencil you can be."

One: "You will be able to do many great things, but

only if you allow yourself to be held in someone's hand."

Two: "You will experience a painful sharpening from time to time, but you'll need it to become a better pencil."

Three: "You will be able to correct any mistakes you might make."

Four: "The most important part of you will always be what's inside."

And Five: "On every surface you are used on, you must leave your mark. No matter what the
Condition, you must continue to write."

The pencil understood and promised to remember, and went into the box with purpose in its heart. Now replacing the place of the pencil with you. Always remember them and never forget, and you will become the best person you can be.

One: "You will be able to do many great things, but only if you allow yourself to be held in God's hand. And allow other human beings to access you for the many gifts you possess."

Two: "You will experience a painful sharpening from time to time, by going through various
Problems in life, but you'll need it to become a stronger person."

Three: "You will be able to correct any mistakes you might make."

Four: "The most important part of you will always be what's on the inside."

And Five: "On every surface you walk through, you must leave your mark. No matter what the situation, you must continue to do your duties."

Allow this parable on the pencil to encourage you to know that you are a special person and only you can fulfill the purpose to which you were born to accomplish.

Never allow yourself to get discouraged and think that Your life is insignificant and cannot make a change.

Two Goats over a Bridge

There was a river in a small village. People use a narrow bridge built over the river to cross it. One day a goat was crossing the bridge. He saw another goat crossing the bridge in the opposite direction. The bridge was so narrow that there was no space for both of them to pass.

Both of the goats didn't want to go back. One goat said to the other goat "You should go back since I am stronger than you". The other goat denied saying it's stronger. Both of them argued for a while. Later, one goat put down his horns to fight to show it is stronger than the other.

They fight furiously and both of them lost their balance and fell into the stream below. The swift current of the stream carried them away in deep water and both of them were drowned.

After a while another two goats came on the same bridge in opposite direction. Both of them started quarrelling that one goat should give way to other. This time one goat thought for a while and asked the other goat to stop. He

said "If we both fight, we will fall into the river and be drowned. Instead I have a plan. I will lie down, and you walk over me." Then the wise goat lay down on the bridge, and the other goat walked over him. So they passed each other, and went on their ways.

Anger leads to sorrow and please leads to joy.

The Wise Cock and the Wicked Fox

There lived a wise cock in a village. He did his duties well. He crowed early in the morning, waking up the folks for their daily chores.

One day, the cock was taking rest on a treetop. A wicked fox passed that way. The fox looked up and saw the handsome cock perched on the tree. The fox decided to eat the cock. So, he said in as sweet a voice as possible, "Hello, dear cock! I bring you news from heaven. There is a new order laid for us. From now on, all birds and animals shall become friends and live together in peace".

The cock was astonished. He asked "Is it true?"

The fox replied, "Yes, of course. If you would like to test it, why not come down?" Now, the cock began to think wise. He said, "Won't you wait a minute. A few of our friends are coming along".

It was the fox's turn to be surprised, "Friends! Who are coming? What do you mean? The cock answered, "I can see some hounds coming. Let us wait for them".

On hearing the words 'Hounds' the fox got

annoyed. He started to run away. The cock asked, "Why are you running? What happened to our friendship?" The only reply was "Forget it".

Be wise when you get surprising information from sudden friends.

THE BOY AND THE APPLE TREE

A long time ago, there was a huge apple tree. A little boy loved to come and play around it every day. He climbed to the treetop, ate the apples, and took a nap under the shadow. He loved the tree and the tree loved to play with him. Time went by, the little boy had grown up and he no longer played around the tree every day.

One day, the boy came back to the tree and he looked sad.
"Come and play with me", the tree asked the boy.
"I am no longer a kid, I do not play around trees anymore" the boy replied.
"I want toys. I need money to buy them."
"Sorry, I do not have money, but you can pick all my apples and sell them. So, you will have money."
The boy was so excited. He grabbed all the apples on the tree and left happily. The boy never came back after he picked the apples.

The tree was sad.

One day, the boy who now turned into a man returned and the tree was excited.
"Come and play with me" the tree said.
"I do not have time to play. I have to work for my family. We need a house for shelter.

Can you help me?"

"Sorry, but I do not have any house. But you can chop off my branches to build your house." So the man cut all the branches of the tree and left happily. The tree was glad to see him happy but the man never came back since then. The tree was again lonely and sad.

One hot summer day, the man returned and the tree was delighted.
"Come and play with me!" the tree said.
"I am getting old. I want to go sailing to relax myself. Can you give me a boat?" said the man.
"Use my trunk to build your boat. You can sail far away and be happy."
So the man cut the tree trunk to make a boat. He went sailing and never showed up for a long time.

Finally, the man returned after many years. "Sorry, my boy. But I do not have anything for you anymore. No more apples for you", the tree said. "No problem, I do not have any teeth to bite" the man replied.

"No more trunk for you to climb on." "I am too old for that now" the man said.

"I really cannot give you anything, the only thing left is my dying roots," the tree said with tears.

"I do not need much now, just a place to rest. I am tired after all these years," the man replied.

"Good! Old tree roots are the best place to lean on and rest, come sit down with me and rest." The man sat down and the tree was glad and smiled with tears.

This is a story of everyone. The tree is like our parents. When we were young, we loved to play with our Mum and Dad. When we grow up, we leave them; only come to them when we need something or when we are in trouble. No matter what, parents will always be there and give everything they could just to make you happy.

You may think the boy is cruel to the tree, but that is how all of us treat our parents. We take them for granted; we don't appreciate all they do for us, until it's too late. Wallahi, May Allah forgives us of our shortcomings and may He guide us.

THE ANGEL

Once upon a time there was a child ready to be born. One day the child asked God, "They tell me you are going to send me to earth tomorrow but how am I going to live there being so small and helpless?" God replied, "Among the many angels I have chosen one for you. She will be waiting for you and will take care of you."

Said child, "But tell me here in Heaven I don't do anything else but sing and smile. That's what I need to be happy!" God replied,

"Your angel will sing for you every day. And you will feel your angel's love and be happy."

And, said the child, "How am I going to be able to understand when people talk to me, if I don't know the language that men talk?" "That's easy", God said, "Your angel will tell you the most beautiful and sweet words you will ever hear, and with much patience and care, your angel will teach you how to speak." The child looked up at God saying, "And what am I going to do when I want to talk to you?" God smiled at the child saying, "Your angel will teach you how to pray."

The child said, "I've heard on earth there are bad men. Who will protect me?" God replied, "Your angel will defend you, even if it means risking life!" The child looked sad, saying, "But I will always be sad because I will not see you anymore." God replied, "Your angel will always talk to you about me and will teach you the way to come back to me, even though I will always be next to you."

At that moment there was much peace in Heaven, but voices from earth could already be heard.

The child in a hurry, asked softly, "Oh God, if I am about to leave now please tell me my angel's name!"

God replied, your angel's name is of no importance... you will simply call her

MOTHER!

THE DEVOTED MOTHER

A mother duck and her little ducklings were on their way to the lake one day. The ducklings were very happy following their mother and quack-quacking along the way.
All of a sudden the mother duck saw a fox in the distance.

She was frightened and shouted, "Children, hurry to the lake. There's a fox!" The ducklings hurried towards the lake. The mother duck wondered what to do. She began to walk back and forth dragging one wing on the ground.

When the fox saw her he became happy. He said to himself, "It seems that she's hurt and can't fly! I can easily catch and eat her!" Then he ran towards her.

The mother duck ran, leading the fox away from the lake. The fox followed her. Now he wouldn't be able to harm her ducklings. The mother duck looked towards her ducklings and saw that they had reached the lake. She was relieved, so she stopped and took a deep breath.

The fox thought she was tired and he came closer, but the mother duck quickly spread her wings and rose up in the air. She landed in the middle of the lake and her ducklings swam to her.

The fox stared in disbelief at the mother duck and her ducklings. He could not reach them because they were in the middle of the lake.

Dear children, some birds drag one of their wings on the ground when an enemy is going to attack. In this way they fool their enemies into thinking they are hurt. When the enemy follows them this gives their children time to escape.

MENTALLY RETARDED!

A few years ago, at the Seattle Special Olympics, nine contestants, all physically or mentally disabled, assembled at the starting line for the 100-yard dash.

At the gun, they all started out, not exactly in a dash, but with a relish to run the race to the finish and win. All, that is, except one little boy who stumbled on the asphalt, tumbled over a couple of times, and began to cry. The other eight heard the boy cry. They slowed down and looked back. Then they all turned around and went back.....every one of them.

One girl with Down's syndrome bent down and kissed him and said, "This will make it better."

Then all nine linked arms and walked together to the finish line. Everyone in the stadium stood, and the cheering went on for several minutes. People who were there are still telling the story.

Why? Because deep down we know this one thing: What matters in this life is more than winning for ourselves. What matters in this life is helping others win, even if it means slowing down and changing our course.

PAID IN FULL

A little boy came up to his mother in the kitchen one evening while she was fixing supper, and he handed her a piece of paper that he had been writing on. After his mom dried her hands on an apron, she read it, and this is what it said:

For cutting the grass: $5.00
For cleaning up my room this week: $1.00
For going to the store for you: $.50
Baby-sitting my kid brother while you went shopping: $.25

Taking out the garbage: $1.00
For getting a good report card: $5.00
For cleaning up and raking the yard: $2.00
Total owed: $14.75

Well, his mother looked at him standing there, and the boy could see the memories flashing through her mind. She picked up the pen, turned over the paper he had written on, and this is what she wrote:

For the nine months I carried you while you were growing inside me: No Charge.

For all the nights that I've sat up with you, doctored and prayed for you: No Charge.

For all the trying times, and all the tears that you've caused through the years: No Charge.

For all the nights filled with dread and for the worries I knew were ahead: No Charge.

For the toys, food, clothes, and even wiping your nose: No Charge.

When you add it up, the cost of my love is: No Charge.

When the boy finished reading what his mother had written, there were big tears in his eyes, and he looked straight up at his mother and said, "Mom, I sure do love you."

And then he took the pen and in great big letters he wrote:

"PAID IN FULL"

Beautiful Gift

A young man was getting ready to graduate college. For many months he had admired a beautiful sports car in a dealer's showroom, and knowing his father could well afford it, he told him that was all he wanted. As Graduation Day approached, the young man awaited signs that his father had purchased the car.

On the morning of his graduation his father called him into his private study.

His father told him how proud he was to have such a fine son, and told him how much he loved him. He handed his son a beautiful wrapped gift box. Curious, but somewhat disappointed the young man opened the box and found a lovely, leather-bound Holy Qur'an. Angrily, he raised his voice at his father and said, "With all your money you give me a Holy book?" and stormed out of the house, leaving the holy book.

He never contacted his father again for long time. Many years passed and the young man was very successful in business. He had a beautiful home and wonderful family, but realized his father was very old, and thought perhaps he should go to him. He had not seen him since that graduation day.

Before he could make arrangements, he received a telegram telling him his father had passed away, and willed all of his possessions to his son. He needed to come home immediately and take care things. When he arrived at his father's house, sudden sadness and regret filled his heart.

He began to search his father's important papers and saw the still new Holy Qur'an, just as he had left it years ago. With tears, he opened the Holy Qur'an and began to turn the pages. As he Read those words, a car key dropped from an envelope taped behind the Holy Qur'an. It had a tag with the dealer's name, the same dealer who had the sports car he had desired.

On the tag was the date of his graduation, and the words PAID IN FULL.

How many times do we miss GOD blessings because they are not packaged as we expected?

WHAT IS A FAMILY?

A man came home from work late, tired and irritated, to find his 5-year old son waiting for him at the door.

SON: "Daddy, may I ask you a question?"

DAD: "Yeah sure, what it is?" replied the man.

SON: "Daddy, how much do you make an hour?"

DAD: "That's none of your business. Why do you ask such a thing?" the man said angrily.

SON: "I just want to know. Please tell me, how much do you make an hour?"

DAD: "If you must know, I make $20 an hour."

"Oh," the little boy replied, with his head down. Looking up, he said,
 "Daddy, may I please borrow $10?"

The father was furious, "If the only reason you asked that is so you can borrow some money to buy a silly toy or some other nonsense, then you march yourself straight to your room and go to bed. Think about why you are being so selfish. I work hard every day for such this childish behavior."

The little boy quietly went to his room and shut the door. The man sat down and started to get even angrier about the little boy's questions. How dare he ask such questions only to get some money?

After about an hour or so, the man had calmed down, and started to think: Maybe there was
something he really needed to buy with that $10 and he really didn't ask for money very often.

The man went to the door of the little boy's room and opened the door.

"Are you asleep, son?" He asked. "No daddy, I'm awake," replied the boy.

"I've been thinking, maybe I was too hard on you earlier," said the man. "It's been a long day and I took out my aggravation on you. Here's the $10 you asked for."

The little boy sat straight up, smiling. "Oh, thank you daddy!" He yelled. Then, reaching under his pillow he pulled out some crumpled up bills.

The man seeing that the boy already had money, started to get angry again. The little boy slowly counted out his money, and then looked up at his father.

"Why do you want more money if you already have some?" the father grumbled.

"Because I didn't have enough, but now I do," the little boy replied.

"Daddy, I have $20 now. Can I buy an hour of your time? Please come home early tomorrow.

I would like to have dinner with you."

Share this story with someone you like.... But even better, share $20 worth of time with someone you love. It's just a short reminder to all of you working so hard in life.

We should not let time slip through our fingers without having spent some time with those who really matter to us, those close to our hearts.

If we die tomorrow, the company that we are working for could easily replace us in a matter of days.

But the family & friends we leave behind will feel the loss for the rest of their lives. And come to think of it, we pour ourselves more into work than to our family. An unwise investment indeed!

So what is the moral of the story???

Don't work too hard...and you know what the full word of FAMILY is?

FAMILY = (F)ATHER (A)ND (M)OTHER,(I)(L)OVE (Y)OU!

TRUE WEALTH

One day a father of a very wealthy family took his son on a trip to the country with the purpose of showing his son how the poor people live so he could be thankful for his wealth.
They spent a couple of days and nights on the farm of what would be considered a very poor family.

On their return from their trip, the father asked his son, "How was the trip?" "It was great, Dad."

"Did you see how poor people can be?" the father asked. "Oh yeah" said the son. "So what did you learn from the trip?" asked the father.

The son answered, "I saw that we have one dog and they had four. We have a pool that reaches to the middle of our garden and they have a creek that has no end." "We have imported lanterns in our garden and they have the stars at night." "Our patio reaches to the front yard and they have the whole horizon." "We have a small piece of land to live on and they have fields that go beyond outsight." "We have servants who serve us, but they serve others."

"We buy our food, but they grow theirs." "We have walls around our property to protect us; they have friends to protect them."

With this the boy's father was speechless. Then his son added, "Thanks dad for showing me how poor we are."

A HOLE IN THE FENCE

There once was a little boy who had a bad temper. His Father gave him a bag of nails and told him that every time he lost his temper, he must hammer a nail into the back of the fence.

The first day the boy had driven 37 nails into the fence. Over the next few weeks, as he learned to control his anger, the number of nails hammered daily gradually dwindled down.

He discovered it was easier to hold his temper than to drive those nails into the fence....

Finally the day came when the boy didn't lose his temper at all. He told his father about it and the father suggested that the boy now pull out one nail for each day that he was able to hold his temper. The day passed and the young boy was finally able to tell his father that all the nails were gone. The father took his son by the hand and led him to the fence. He said, "You have done well, my son, but look at the holes in the fence."

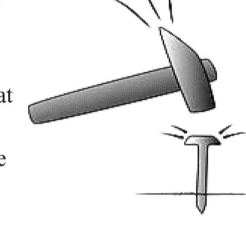

The fence will never be the same. When you say things in anger, they leave a scar just like this one.

You can put a knife in a man and draw it out. It won't matter how many times you say I'm sorry, the wound is still there. **A verbal wound is as bad as a physical one.**

Friends and loved ones is a very rare jewel, indeed. They make you smile and encourage you to succeed. They lend an ear, they share a word of praise, and they always want to open their hearts to us. Water your relationships with kindness... and they will grow. So be careful little lips what you say...! And you won't chase friendships away.

GRANDPA'S TABLE

A frail old man went to live with his son, daughter-in-law, and four-year old grandson. The old man's hands trembled, his eyesight was blurred, and his step faltered. The family ate together at the table.

"Little Things Affect Little Minds"
BENJAMIN DISRAELI

But the elderly grandfather's shaky hands and failing sight made eating difficult. Peas
rolled off his spoon onto the floor. When he grasped, the glass, milk spilled on the tablecloth.

The son and daughter-in-law became irritated with the mess. "We must do something about Grandfather," said the son. "I've had enough of his spilled milk, noisy eating, and food on the floor." So the husband and wife set a small table in the corner.

There, Grandfather ate alone while the rest of the family enjoyed dinner. Since Grandfather had broken a dish or two, his food was served in a wooden bowl. When the family glanced in Grandfather's direction, sometimes he had a tear in his eye as he sat alone. Still, the only words the couple had for him were sharp admonitions when he dropped a fork or spilled food. The four-year-old watched it all in silence.

One evening before supper, the father noticed his son playing with wood scraps on the floor. He asked the child sweetly, "What are you making?" Just as sweetly, the boy  responded, "Oh, I am making a little bowl for you and Mama to eat your food in when I grow up." The four-year-old smiled and went back to work. The words so struck the parents that they were speechless. Then tears started to stream down their cheeks. Though no word was spoken, both knew what must be done.

That evening the husband took Grandfather's hand and gently led him back to the family table.

For the remainder of his days he ate every meal with the family. And for some reason, neither husband nor wife seemed to care any longer when a fork was dropped, milk spilled, or the tablecloth soiled.

Children are remarkably perceptive. Their eyes ever observe, their ears ever listen, and their minds ever process the messages they absorb. If they see us patiently provide a happy home atmosphere for family members, they will imitate that attitude for the rest of their lives. The wise parent realizes that every day the building blocks are being laid for the child's future. Let's be wise builders and role models.

"Life is about people connecting with people, and making a positive difference.
Take care of yourself,… and those you love, … today, … and every day!"

FATHERS EYES

A teenager lived alone with his father, and the two of them had a very special relationship. The father believed in encouragement. Even though the son was always on the bench, his father was always in the stands cheering. He never missed a game.

This young man was the smallest of the class when he entered high school. His father continued to encourage him but also made it very clear that he did not have to play football if he didn't want to.

But the young man loved football and decided to hang in there. He was determined to try his best at every practice, and perhaps he'd get to play when he became a senior. All through high school he never missed a practice or a game, but remained a bench warmer all four years. His faithful father was always in the stands, always with words of encouragement for him. When the young man went to college, he decided to try out for the football team as a "walk-on."

Everyone was sure he could never make the cut, but he did. The coach admitted that he kept him on the roster because he always puts his heart and soul to every practice, and at the same time, provided the other members with the spirit and hustle they badly needed.

The news that he had survived the cut thrilled him so much that he rushed to the nearest phone and called his father.

His father shared his excitement and was sent season tickets for all the college games. This persistent young athlete never missed practice during his four years at college, but he never got to play in the game.

It was the end of his senior football season, and as he trotted onto the practice field shortly before the big play-off game, the coach met him with a telegram. The young man read the telegram and he became deathly silent. Swallowing hard, he mumbled to the coach, "My father died this morning.

Is it all right if I miss practice today?"

The coach put his arm gently around his shoulder and said, "Take the rest of the week off, son. And don't even plan to come back to the game on Saturday." Saturday arrived, and the game was not going well.

In the third quarter, when the team was ten points behind, a silent young man quietly slipped into the empty locker room and put on his football gear. As he ran onto the sidelines, the coach and his players were astounded to see their faithful team-mate back so soon.

"Coach, please let me play. I've just got to play today," said the young man. The coach pretended not to hear him. There was no way he wanted his worst player in this close playoff game. But the young man persisted, and finally feeling sorry for the kid, the coach gave in.

"All right," he said. "You can go in." Before long, the coach, the players and everyone in the stands could not believe their eyes. This little unknown, who had never played before, was doing everything right. The opposing team could not stop him. He ran, he passed, blocked and tackled like a star. His team began to triumph.

The score was soon tied. In the closing seconds of the game, this kid intercepted a pass and ran all the way for the winning touchdown. The fans broke loose. His team-mates hoisted him onto their shoulders. Such cheering you've never heard!

Finally, after the stands had emptied and the team had showered and left the locker room, the coach noticed that the young man was sitting quietly in the corner all alone. The coach came to him and said, "Kid, I can't believe it. You were fantastic!"

Tell me what got into you? How did you do it? He looked at the coach, with tears in his eyes, and said,

"Well, you knew my dad died, but did you know that my dad was blind?" The young man swallowed hard and forced a smile, "Dad came to all my games, but today
was the first time he could see me play, and I wanted to show him I could do it!"

BUTTERFLY AND COCOON

A man found a cocoon of a butterfly. One day a small opening appeared; he sat and watched the butterfly for several hours as it struggled to force its body through that little hole. Then it seemed to stop making any progress. It appeared as if it had gotten as far as it could and it could go no farther.

Then the man decided to help the butterfly, so he took a pair of scissors and snipped off the remaining bit of the

cocoon. The butterfly then emerged easily. But it had a swollen body and small, shriveled wings.

The man continued to watch the butterfly because he expected that, at any moment, the wings would enlarge and expand to be able to support the body, which would contract in time.

Neither happened! In fact, the butterfly spent the rest of its life crawling around with a swollen body and shriveled wings. It never was able to fly. What this man in his kindness and haste did not understand was that the restricting cocoon and the struggle required for the butterfly to get through the tiny opening were nature's way of forcing fluid from the body of the butterfly into its wings so that it would be ready for flight once it achieved its freedom from the cocoon.

Sometimes struggles are exactly what we need in our life. If nature allowed us to go through our life without any obstacles, it would cripple us. We would not be as strong as what we could have been. And we could never fly...

THE OBSTACLE IN OUR PATH

In ancient times, a king had a boulder placed on a roadway. Then he hid himself and watched to see if anyone would remove the huge rock. Some of the king's wealthiest merchants and courtiers came by and simply walked around it.

Many loudly blamed the king for not keeping the roads clear, but none did anything about getting the big stone out of the way. Then a peasant came along carrying a load of vegetables.

On approaching the boulder, the peasant laid down his burden and tried to move the stone to the side of the road. After much pushing and straining, he finally succeeded. As the peasant picked up his load of vegetables, he noticed a purse lying in the road where the boulder had been.

The purse contained many gold coins and a note from the king indicating that the gold was for the person who removed the boulder from the roadway. The peasant learned what many others never understand.

Every obstacle presents an opportunity to improve one's condition.

THE WOLF IN SHEEP'S CLOTHING

A Wolf found great difficulty in getting at the sheep owing to the vigilance of the shepherd and his dogs. But one day it found the skin of a sheep that had been flayed and thrown aside, so it put it on over its own pelt and strolled down among the sheep. The

Lamb that belonged to the sheep, whose skin the Wolf was wearing, began to follow the Wolf in the Sheep's clothing; so, leading the Lamb a little apart, he soon made a meal off her, and for some time he succeeded in deceiving the sheep, and enjoying hearty meals.

Appearances are deceptive.

DON'T JUDGE A BOOK BY ITS COVER!

A lady in a faded gingham dress and her husband, dressed in a homespun threadbare suit, stepped off the train in Boston and walk timidly without an appointment into the Harvard University President's outer office.

The secretary could tell in a moment that such backwoods, country hicks had no business at Harvard and probably didn't even deserve to be in Cambridge.

"We want to see the president," the man said softly.

"He'll be busy all day," the secretary snapped.

"We'll wait," the lady replied.

For hours the secretary ignored them, hoping that the couple would finally become discouraged and go away. They didn't and the secretary grew frustrated and finally decided to disturb the president, even though it was a chore she always regretted.

"Maybe if you see them for a few minutes, they'll leave," she said to him. He sighed in exasperation and nodded. Someone of his importance obviously didn't have the time to spend with them, but he detested gingham dresses and homespun suits cluttering up his outer office.

The president, stern faced and with dignity, strutted toward the couple. The lady told him, "We had a son who attended Harvard for one year. He loved Harvard. He was happy here.

But about a year ago, he was accidentally killed. My husband and I would like to erect a memorial to him, somewhere on campus."

The president wasn't touched.... He was shocked.

"Madam," he said, gruffly, "we can't put up a statue for every person who attended Harvard and died. If we did, this place would look like a cemetery." "Oh, no," the lady explained quickly. "We don't want to erect a statue. We thought we would like to give a building to

Harvard."

The president rolled his eyes. He glanced at the gingham dress and homespun suit, and then exclaimed, "A building! Do you have any earthly idea how much a building costs? We have over seven and a half million dollars in the physical buildings here at Harvard."

For a moment the lady was silent.

The president was pleased. Maybe he could get rid of them now. The lady turned to her husband and said quietly, "Is that all it costs to start a university? Why don't we just start our own?"

Her husband nodded.

The president's face wilted in confusion and bewilderment. Mr. and Mrs. Leland Stanford got up and walked away, traveling to Palo Alto, California where they established the University that bears their name, Stanford University, a memorial to a son that Harvard no longer cared about.

You can easily judge the character of others by how they treat those who they think can do nothing.

MOUNTAIN STORY

A son and his father were walking on the mountains. Suddenly, his son falls, hurts himself and screams: "AAAhhhhhhhhhhh!"

To his surprise, he hears the voice repeating, somewhere in the mountain: "AAAhhhhhhhhhh!"

Curious, he yells: "Who are you?"

He receives the answer: "Who are you?"

And then he screams to the mountain: "I admire you!"

The voice answers: "I admire you!"

Angered at the response, he screams: "Coward!"

He receives the answer: "Coward!"

He looks to his father and asks: "What's going on?"

The father smiles and says: "My son, pay attention."

Again the man screams: "You are a champion!"

The voice answers: "You are a champion!"

The boy is surprised, but does not understand.

Then the father explains: "People call this ECHO, but really this is LIFE."

It gives you back everything you say or do. Our life is simply a reflection of our actions. If you want more love in the world, create more love in your heart.

If you want more competence in your team, improve your competence.

This relationship applies to everything, in all aspects of life; Life will give you back everything you have given to it."

"Your life is not a coincidence. It's a reflection of you!"

A LESSON FROM A FROG TALE

A group of frogs were hopping contentedly through the woods, going about their Froggy business, when two of them fell into a deep pit. All of the other frogs gathered around the pit to see what could be done to help their companions. When they saw how deep the pit was, the rest of the dismayed group agreed that it was hopeless and told the two frogs in the pit that they should prepare themselves for their fate, because they were as good as dead.

Unwilling to accept this terrible fate, the two frogs began to jump with all of their might. Some of the frogs shouted into the pit that it was hopeless, and that the two frogs wouldn't be in that situation if they had been more careful, more obedient to the froggy rules, and more responsible.

The other frogs continued sorrowfully shouting that they should save their energy and give up, since they were already as good as dead. The two frogs continued jumping as hard as they could, and after several hours of desperate effort were quite weary.

Finally, one of the frogs took heed to the calls of his fellows. Spent and disheartened, he quietly resolved himself to his fate, lay down at the bottom of the pit, and died as the others looked on in helpless grief. The other frog continued to jump with every ounce of energy he had, although his body was wracked with pain and he was completely exhausted.

His companions began a new, yelling for him to accept his fate, stop the pain and just die. The weary frog jumped harder and harder and - wonder of wonders! Finally leapt so high that he sprang from the pit. Amazed, the other  frogs celebrated his miraculous freedom and then gathering around him asked,

"Why did you continue jumping when we told you it was impossible?" Reading their lips, the astonished frog explained to them that he was deaf and that when he saw their gestures and shouting, he thought they were cheering him on. What he had perceived as encouragement inspired him to try harder and to succeed against all odds.

This simple story contains a powerful lesson. Your encouraging words can lift someone up and help him or her make it through the day. Your destructive words can cause deep wounds; they may be the weapons that destroy someone's desire to continue trying - or even their life. Your destructive, careless word can diminish someone in the eyes of others, destroy their influence and have a lasting impact on the way others respond to them.

WEAKNESS OR STRENGTH?

Sometimes your biggest weakness can become your biggest strength. Take, for example, the story of one 10-year-old boy who decided to study Judo despite the fact that he had lost his left arm in a devastating car accident.

The boy began lessons with an old Japanese Judo Master Sensei.

The boy was doing well, so he couldn't understand why, after three months of training the master had taught him only one move.

"Sensei," the boy finally said, "Shouldn't I be learning more moves?"

"This is the only move you know, but this is the only move you'll ever need to know," the Sensei replied.

Not quite understanding, but believing in his teacher, the boy kept training.

Several months later, the Sensei took the boy to his first tournament. Surprising himself, the boy easily won his first two matches. The third match proved to be more difficult, but after some time, his opponent became impatient and charged; the boy deftly used his one move to win the match.

Still amazed by his success, the boy was now in the finals.

This time, his opponent was bigger, stronger, and more experienced. For a while, the boy appeared to be overmatched. Concerned that the boy might get hurt, the referee called a time-out.

He was about to stop the match when the sensei intervened. "No," the Sensei insisted, "Let him continue."

Soon after the match resumed, his opponent made a critical mistake: he dropped his guard.

Instantly, the boy used his move to pin him. The boy had won the match and the tournament.

He was the champion.

On the way home, the boy and Sensei reviewed every move in each and every match.

Then the boy summoned the courage to ask what was really on his mind.

"Sensei, how did I win the tournament with only one move?"

"You won for two reasons," the Sensei answered. "First, you've almost mastered one of the most difficult throws in all of Judo. And second, the only known defense for that move is for your opponent to grab your left arm."

The boy's biggest weakness had become his biggest strength.

JUST P.U.S.H!

A man was sleeping at night in his cabin when suddenly his room filled with light, and the Lord told the man he had work for him to do, and showed him a large rock in front of his cabin.

The Lord explained that the man was to push against the rock with all his might. So, this the man did, day after day. For many years he toiled from sun up to sun down; his shoulders set squarely against the cold, massive surface of the unmoving rock, pushing with all of his might. Each night the man returned to his cabin sore and worn out, feeling that his whole day had been spent in vain.

Since the man was showing discouragement, the Adversary (Satan) decided to enter the picture by placing thoughts into the weary mind: "you have been pushing against that rock for a long time, and it hasn't moved.

" Thus, giving the man the impression that the task was impossible and that he was a failure. These thoughts discouraged and disheartened the man. Satan said, "Why kill yourself over this?"

"Just put in your time, giving just the minimum effort; and that will be good enough."
That's what he planned to do, but decided to make it a matter of prayer and take his troubled thoughts to the Lord. "Lord," he said, "I have labored long and hard in your service, putting all my strength to do that which you have asked. Yet, after all this time, I have not even budged that rock by half a millimeter. What is wrong? Why am I failing?"

The Lord responded compassionately, "My Servant, when I asked you to serve me and you accepted, I told you that your task was to push against the rock with all of your strength, which you have done. Never once did I mention to you that I expected you to move it. Your task was to push.

And now you come to me with your strength spent, thinking that you have failed. But, is that really so? Look at yourself. Your arms are strong and muscled, your back sinewy and brown, your hands are callused from constant pressure, and your legs have become massive and hard.

Through opposition you have grown much, and your abilities now surpass that which you used to have. Yet you haven't moved the rock. But your calling was to be obedient and to push and to exercise your faith and trust in my wisdom. This you have done.

Now I, my servant, will move the rock." At times, when we hear a word from God, we tend to use our own intellect to decipher what He wants, when actually what God wants is just a simple obedience and faith in Him. By all means, exercise the faith that moves mountains, but know that it is still God who moves mountains.

When everything seems to go wrong .... just P.U.S.H!
When the job gets you down... just P.U.S.H!
When people don't react the way you think they should..... just P.U.S.H!

When your money is "gone" and the bills are due.............. just P.U.S.H!
When people just don't understand you .... just P.U.S.H!

$P + U + S + H = Pray + Until + Something + Happens$

DETERMINATON

In 1883, a creative engineer named John Roebling was inspired by an idea to build a spectacular bridge connecting New York with the Long Island. However bridge building experts throughout the world thought that this was an impossible feat and told Roebling to forget the idea. It just could not be done. It was not practical. It had never been done before.

Roebling could not ignore the vision he had in his mind of this bridge. He thought about it all the time and he knew deep in his heart that it could be done. He just had to share the dream with someone else. After much discussion and persuasion he managed to convince his son Washington, an up and coming engineer, that the bridge in fact could be built.

Working together for the first time, the father and son developed concepts of how it could be accomplished and how the obstacles could be overcome. With great excitement and inspiration, and the headiness of a wild challenge before them, they hired their crew and began to build their dream bridge.

The project started well, but when it was only a few months underway a tragic accident on the site took the life of John Roebling. Washington was injured and left with a certain amount of brain damage, which resulted in him not being able to walk or talk or even move.

"We told them so."
"Crazy men and their crazy dreams."
"It's foolish to chase wild visions."

Everyone had a negative comment to make and felt that the project should be scrapped since the Roebling's were the only ones who knew how the bridge could be built. In spite of his handicap Washington was never discouraged and still had a burning desire to complete the bridge and his mind was still as sharp as ever.

He tried to inspire and pass on his enthusiasm to some of his friends, but they were too daunted by the task. As he lay on his bed in his hospital room, with the sunlight streaming through the windows, a gentle breeze blew the flimsy white curtains apart and he was able to see the sky and the tops of the trees outside for just a moment.

It seemed that there was a message for him not to give up. Suddenly an idea hit him. All he could do was move one finger and he decided to make the best use of it. By moving this, he slowly developed a code of communication with his wife.

He touched his wife's arm with that finger, indicating to her that he wanted her to call the
engineers again. Then he used the same method of tapping her arm to tell the engineers what to do.

It seemed foolish but the project was under way again.

For 13 years Washington tapped out his instructions with his finger on his wife's arm, until the bridge was finally completed. Today the spectacular Brooklyn Bridge stands in all its glory as a tribute to the triumph of one man's indomitable spirit and his determination not to be defeated by circumstances. It is also a tribute to the engineers and their team work, and to their faith in a man who was considered mad by half the world. It stands too as a tangible monument to the love and devotion of his wife who for 13 long years patiently decoded the messages of her husband and told the engineers what to do.

Perhaps this is one of the best examples of a never-say-die attitude that overcomes a terrible physical handicap and achieves an impossible goal.

Often when we face obstacles in our day-to-day life, our hurdles seem very small in comparison to what many others have to face.

The Brooklyn Bridge shows us that dreams that seem impossible can be realized with determination and persistence, no matter what the odds are.

Even the most distant dream can be realized with determination and persistence.

THE CRACKED POT

Once upon a time there was a water-bearer in India who had two large pots, each hung on each end of a pole which he carried across his neck. One of the pots had a crack in it, and while the other pot was perfect and always delivered a full portion of water at the end of the long walk from the stream to the master's house, the cracked pot arrived only half full.

For a full two years this went on daily, with the bearer delivering only one and a half pot full of water in his master's house.

Of course, the perfect pot was proud of its accomplishments, perfect to the end for which it was made. But the poor cracked pot was ashamed of its own imperfection, and miserable that it was able to accomplish only half of what it had been made to do.

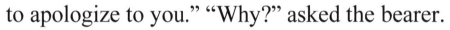

After two years of what it perceived to be a bitter failure, it spoke to the water-bearer one day by the stream. "I am ashamed of myself, and I want to apologize to you." "Why?" asked the bearer. "What are you ashamed of?"

"I have been able, for these past two years, to deliver only half my load because this crack in my side causes water to leak out all the way back to your master's house. Because of my flaws, you have to do all of this work and you don't get full value from your efforts, the pot said. The water-bearer felt sorry for the old cracked pot, and in his compassion he said, "As we return to the master's house, I want you to notice the beautiful flowers along the path."

Indeed, as they went up the hill, the old cracked pot took notice of the sun warming the beautiful wild flowers on the side of the path, and this cheered it some.

But at the end of the trail, it still felt bad because it had leaked out half its load, and so again it apologized to the bearer for its failure.

The bearer said to the pot, "Did you notice that there were flowers only on your side of your path, but not on the other pot's side?

That's because have always known about your flaw, and I took advantage of it. I planted flower seeds on your side of the path, and every day while we walk back from the stream, you've watered them. For two years I have been able to pick these beautiful flowers to decorate my master's table.

Without you being just the way you are, he would not have this beauty to grace his house."

Each of us has our own unique flaw. But it's the cracks and flaws we each have that make our lives together so very interesting and warding. You've just got to take each person for what they are and look for the good in them.

GOD EXISTS

A man went to a barbershop to have his hair and his beard cut as always. He started to have a good conversation with the barber who attended him. They talked about so many things on various subjects.

Suddenly, they touched the subject of God. The barber said: "Look man, I don't believe that God exists as you say so." "Why do you say that?"

Asked the client .Well, it's so easy; you just have to go out in the street to realize that God does not exist. Oh, tell me, if God existed, would there be so many sick people? Would there be abandoned children? If God existed, there would be neither suffering nor pain. "I can't think of a God who permits all of these things." The client stopped for a moment thinking but he didn't want to respond so as to prevent an argument.

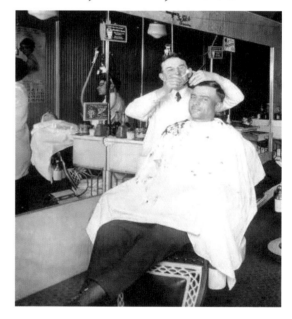

The barber finished his job and the client went out of the shop. Just after he left the barbershop, he saw a man in the street with a long hair and beard (it seems that it had been a long time since he had his cut and he looked so untidy). Then the client again entered the barbershop and he said to the barber: "know what? Barbers do not exist."

"How come they don't exist?" asked the barber. "Well I am here and I am a barber." "No!" – the client exclaimed. "They don't exist because if they did there would be no people with long hair and beard like that man who walks in the street."

"Ah, barbers do exist, what happens is that people do not come to us." "Exactly!" - Affirmed the client. "That's the point. God does exist, what happens is people don't go to Him and do not look for Him that's why there's so much pain and suffering in the world."

A BOY WITH STRONG BELIEF

Shaykh Fath al-Mowsily relates, once I saw a young boy walking through the jungle. It appeared as if he was uttering some words. I greeted him with Salaam and he replied accordingly. I inquired,

"Where are you going?" He retorted, "To the house of Allah (Makkah)." I further asked,

"What are you reciting?"

"The Qur'an" he replied. I remarked, "You are at a tender age, it is not an obligation that you are required to fulfill."
He said, "I have witnessed death approach people younger than me and therefore would like to prepare if death was to knock on my door." I astoundingly commented, "Your steps are small and your destination far." He responded, "My duty is to take the step and it remains the responsibility of Allah to take me to my destination." I continued to ask,

"Where your provision and conveyance is (means of transport)."

He replied, "My Yaqeen (belief) is my provision and my feet's are my conveyance." I explained, "I am asking you regarding bread and water."

He replied! "Oh Shaykh if someone invited you to his house, would it be appropriate to take your own food?" I exclaimed, "No!" "Similarly, My Lord has invited His servant to His house; it is only the weakness of your Yaqeen that makes us carry

provisions. Despite this, do you think Allah will let me go to waste?" "Never" I replied. He then left. Sometime later I saw him in Makkah. He approached me and inquired, "Oh Shaykh are you still of weak belief?"

Source: Stories of the Pious by Shaikh Ahmad Ali

THE ONE-EYED DOE

A Doe had the misfortune to lose one of her eyes, and could not see any one approaching her on that side. So to avoid any danger she always used to feed on a high cliff near the sea, with her sound eye looking towards the land. By this means she could see whenever the hunters approached her on land, and often escaped by this means. But the hunters found out that she was blind of one eye, and hiring a boat rowed under the cliff where she used to

feed and shot her from the sea. "Ah," cried she with her dying voice.

"You cannot escape your fate."

A MERCHANT AND HIS DONKEY

One beautiful spring morning, a merchant loaded his donkey with
bags of salt to go to the market in order to sell them. The merchant and his donkey were walking along together.

They had not walked far when they reached a river on the road.

Unfortunately, the donkey slipped and fell into the river and noticed that the bags of salt loaded on his back became lighter.

There was nothing the merchant could do, except return home where he loaded his donkey with more bags of salt. As they reached the slippery riverbank, now deliberately, the  donkey fell into the river and wasted all the bags of salt on its back again.

The merchant quickly discovered the donkey's trick. He then returned home again but re-loaded his donkey with bags of sponges.

The foolish, tricky donkey again set on its way. On reaching the river he again fell into the water. But instead of the load becoming lighter, it became heavier.

The merchant laughed at him and said: "You foolish donkey, your trick had been discovered, you should know that, those who are too clever sometimes over reach themselves."

CPSIA information can be obtained at www.ICGtesting.com
Printed in the USA
BVIW121627101120
592969BV00025B/20